Chalet Fields of the Gower

Photographs by Stefan Szczelkun

An interview with
architect Owen Short

2nd Expanded Edition
Routine Art Co.   2018

ISBN: 978-1-870736-16-9

All Rights Reserved

Interview with architect Owen Short – Part 1 Sandy Lane

Owen: My father was an estate agent and he must have had some business in one of the chalet fields: I needed a new push-bike and he located one in a chalet somewhere: I accompanied him in the car to collect this lovely racing bike [it had a fixed wheel – which has recently become real trendy – but I was the only person I knew who had a fixed wheel bike]. I remember going into this slightly unusual area where all the houses were made of wood – as I would have described them then – and I was probably about ten.

Stefan: So that was in the Fifties?

Owen: Yes. My next recollection I have of them was… having moved to Mumbles just about the time of my thirteenth birthday, one of the guys I got to know lived in one of the chalet fields. It was called a field but it was a cinder track with a hedge on one side and a row of chalets on the other side. That was Rosser's Field in Limeslade. So, having a friend living there we visited quite often. Off the main road - Plunch Lane - up from Limeslade beach, there were different types of shacks and shanties all the way up on both sides. I particularly remember them because some of them were octagonal. Looking back, they were obviously prefabricated for export somewhere. I thought they were most interesting.

Not long after that my Father actually bought a chalet that was right in the heart of Mumbles just behind the rugby club where one of the steep hills goes up to come out at Thistleboon, which connects with Limeslade which is on the other side of the hill. In Mumbles Village there were a couple of little smatterings of chalets. He bought one, which was called 'Wood Edge'. It was number 22A Western Lane. There were four or five chalets there, but there was no road access to them. Western Lane was very, very steep and narrow - it has since become one way and restricted access. There was a two-car parking space at the entrance but that belonged to one chalet in particular. Sometimes we would park there and dash in. This chalet was in rather poor condition and my Mother didn't like that so she didn't have any particular inkling to go there on the weekend [they had a town house in Swansea]. Later on, when Clive Sinclair devised the Sinclair C5 – the little electric tricycle – my Father bought one because he thought that would help him get building materials and things into the site, because it was so difficult to do it any other way. (The C5 was assembled in Merthyr Tydfil) Eventually after my Dad died in 1985 my Mum decided to dispose of the plot. In the meantime, I'd got planning permission to build a new chalet on the plot.

Stefan: You'd also been away to The School of Architecture in Portsmouth….

Owen: Yes, I was there between 1964 and 1971. Michael, a current colleague, bought the plot off my Mum. I'd known him because we worked in an architect's office in Mumbles. He'd got a job as a kitchen designer and he was persuaded by his girlfriend's Father - who was one of the partners in the office I was working in - to start in the office then go to the school of architecture in Cardiff. He bought the plot and designed and built a modern version of a timber chalet.

Stefan: How had that awareness come about? Instead of the common practice of buying one and knocking it down to build a standard brick bungalow.

Owen: I dunno, we can ask him [Laughs]. It was difficult to get materials in there so he wanted to build it as a timber frame which was easy to carry there in bits, rather than thousands of bricks and bags of cement. He had a builder friend that attended the same church as him and I think he built it all almost single-handedly in about six months. It was basically single-storey with a forty-five degree pitch roof, because it was supposed to be a bungalow – but he sneaked some galleries in at high level. It was built on eight or ten concrete bucket pads with a post coming off each one and then infilled with a timber frame. It was a lovely job.

Stefan: When did you next get involved with converting, repairing or changing chalets?

Owen: Probably after I bought the chalet on Hareslade, which I bought after I fell off my motorbike in 1990. In the office where I was working – where Michael was working when he wasn't in college in Cardiff – they got a few commissions from Sandy Lane where people were beginning to realise the quality of the environment that they could have there for what was a ridiculously cheap amount of money at the time. A friend of mine bought one – probably in the Seventies – for about £120! [Laughs]. He just dug a big hole for drainage…. they didn't have much in way of mains services, especially drains, but it was just up from Three Cliffs Bay, it's pretty sandy soil… That's why it was called Sandy Lane! He was really chuffed because he sold it for £400! [Laughs] And now they are going for £400,000 - partly because they have mostly become freehold properties.

Sandy Lane was, I think, owned by one of the local farms. There's about a hundred or more properties there I think. There would probably have been two hundred there in its heyday. I expect it was a nice little earner for the farmer if he was getting a tenner a year from, perhaps, two hundred (plots) in return for minimal provision of facilities. The site was then bought by a big development group. I think it was BJC who was a big developer in the area at the time. The BJC Group – I think – bought it hoping they could clear the chalets and get planning permission for housing. I can't remember the details, but they were either told there was no way they would get permission to build 'proper' housing there or they were warned not to evict the existing tenants and cause homelessness. Anyway, they decided to abandon the idea and sell the freeholds. That's where Rob Ladds lives. I helped him design his and he wanted to build a traditional timber frame out of massive timbers with complex joints. It was quite an interesting exercise to find out about these things.

Owen: Rob's chalet is all completely new. When he bought it, it was still the old original chalet with a pitched roof. I think it had lost its veranda but there were vestiges of it on the south front there. Very poor condition, but like a lot of them they extend at the back with a very shallow almost flat roof. They go as far back as they can until it runs out of headroom. And it was very much like that and in poor condition. He made the front part habitable and then we designed this whole frame with a central post. He built it in four quarters. So, he built a back quarter first and then the second back quarter. And then when that was all habitable he renewed the front two quarters. All done without permission. He built it as if he was 'repairing' bit by bit. But then when he wanted to put the new roof on – it had a traditional roof with a front-to-back slope – he did go for planning permission.

Owen: I think I probably did the drawings for that as well – I can't remember – with that huge glazed gable facing South. And then he rebuilt some of those lean-to bits. It has a lovely quality inside. It's very difficult to define what makes the quality of chalets so different to ordinary houses! The layouts are usually much less formal. You walk into one of the main rooms rather than into a hall or a corridor. Rob hasn't got a 'front' door because one door goes into his kitchen and the patio doors go straight into the main living room. There's no formal entrance where people would come in.

Stefan: The structure is nothing like the typical shanty.

Owen: No. It's what you would call an English timber frame. I'm not quite sure why English rather than British. Those properly cut joints and different housings - it was quite fun researching.

Stefan: He was a carpenter?

Owen: No, he just got on with it. He wasn't a carpenter. He was a botanist who became an acupuncturist and herbalist which he practiced for many years. He now just grows herbs for the Chinese herbal trade.

Stefan: Sandy Lane is next to one of the most spectacular bays in the Gower. (Interview 2015. Photographs 2013)

The Sandy Lane Community Noticeboard

This was a surviving example of an original chalet.

This is the shed of the red chalet on the right.

This one is still occupied although ramshackle…

This one has a sea view.

Three Cliffs Bay, which is below the Sandy Lane Chalet Field.

Interview Part 2 - Hareslade Chalet Field

Owen: In Hareslade chalet field the land is divided into two. The front field is held freehold by a company which consists of all the individual plot-holders in the front field who each become a 'director' of the company. So, it's allegedly a democratic system. There's some sort of committee that runs the company and grants a lease to each of the individual plot-holders, and then the field – which is still an open space – is shared for use equally. According to Matt [pp58 - 64] some of the more enlightened newcomers, rather than the entrenched old timers, tried to reach an agreement to have a common area where they can do some earthworks with a fire pit in the middle, a play area for kids and such things. But to date they haven't managed to achieve any consensus about exactly what to do with it, so it's just a big space that gets mowed at common expense. The backfield is divided into strips, which are all individually owned freeholds which were acquired from the original land owner. Not everybody could afford to pay – I think it was about £200 that each plot paid the land-owner – and so some people put money in for those who didn't actually have the ready cash for the whole deal to go through. Some of the people who lived there were quite poor and some were crooks and the like. There are all sorts of people! A trust fund or something was set up so the people who couldn't afford to pay at the outset could pay into it and gradually reduce their debt, and eventually everybody would get paid back.

Stefan: When was the Chalet Field at Hareslade first started? Do you know the history of it? Because the Plotlands in England go back to the 1920's.

Owen: No, I don't know the date when it was started. I'm fairly certain that as people slowly got slightly more mobile and had more leisure they were building chalets as holiday homes. A lot of them had no tenure at all. You would rent the ground and build your shack and you had no long-term tenure on the land. There used to be a nominal pound a year annual licence, just to keep it legal, but that gradually changed. In the Sixties, Swansea Council did have a policy of getting rid of them. They decided to take a more positive attitude - in 1973, I think it was. They were getting planning applications in from people who were living in these structures permanently, to alter and extend them. They realised that they couldn't turf these people out, especially as some of them, as in

Hareslade, had become freehold properties by that time. And that's when they actually wrote the planning guidelines. The Design Guide specifically covered Hareslade and Sandy Lane, and specified various things such as what could be built, what happened where a chalet had vanished and other such matters.

Stefan: So, it was a significant moment in the relation between the self-builders and the planning authorities really.

Owen: That Design Guide is still SPG – Special Planning Guidance. More recently there is also a Guide for The Gower, which has been designated an area of outstanding natural beauty.

The Hareslade Design Guide [leafs through a copy] says in its report to committee that they accepted that they could no longer reasonably follow the policy of getting rid of the chalets - which they had done because the chalet fields often had very poor drainage, very poor water supply and no electrical supply. A few of them, as far as I'm aware, still don't have mains electricity, like some of the ones in Caswell. But people were still living in them and wanted to maintain them. The Design Guide said that if one had vanished then you couldn't replace it. If you'd perhaps bought a couple together and knocked one down and so you were using a double or even a treble plot, you couldn't revert to replacing the original separate plots as they became more valuable, which is what people would have tried to do. The Design Guide gave size limits and said they had to look like chalets.

Stefan: What kinds of people were living in Hareslade at the time. Were people living there from the Thirties or whenever it started?

Owen: I don't know anyone that old that is still there. I was aware of Hareslade. I probably used to go there to buy weed or something in the Eighties or before.

Stefan: So, the place had people who lived an 'alternative' lifestyle.

Owen: They were perhaps more alternative then than they are today. There's more professional people living there now.

Stefan: That's only part of it though. When I visited last year, there was a very traditional looking family at the end of the South Field. They didn't want their chalet photographed: "No, No, No! We don't want any publicity!" Which is very common in plotlands because anything that brings attention to them could invite the unwanted attention of the authorities.

Owen: Well it was a complete mixture of some old established families and some druggy types and some hippy types. The chap I bought mine from – not quite sure why he moved out, perhaps it was in too poor condition for him to carry on living in – he got a Housing Association flat. But he was allegedly famous for his consumption of various substances and he was a night bird. But he was a mechanic. He would mend local peoples' cars. Somebody once told me that they were going on a driving holiday and he promised he would service their car before they went. The evening before they went he still hadn't done it so they came and asked him and he said: "Don't worry! Don't worry". He did it over-night. It was ready for them when they needed it. There were all sorts of different characters.

I rediscovered Hareslade because, when I did the Flats at 550 in The Mumbles – where you came to stay once – Neil who bought the upstairs flat was in partnership with his lady friend. They split up and he had a colleague in work whose wife's family had a chalet in the front field. I'm not quite sure how, but anyhow, Neil was able to get his hands on this and I went to visit him there and he was doing a lot of work on this chalet and he'd stuck an extra level in. You were never allowed to have a second storey. They had to be just single storey. Though they couldn't stop people putting Velux windows in the roof and colonising the attic space. But the rear wing of this one had a spiral staircase that went up to an illegal bedroom under the roof of the wing at the back. Neil had put a dormer window in, which couldn't be seen from anywhere public. But the planners turned up and told him to take it down because it was too overtly a second storey.

I'd never really fancied living in one of the chalets previously because, although my Dad had bought one, it was very much a hobby for him. His plot must have been freehold because, being an estate agent, he told me that most of these places have no value at all if you've got no tenure on the land. If you don't pay your annual rent or something you could lose everything. But anyhow by 1994 I'd changed my attitude towards them and discovered there was an empty one in the back field of Hareslade. People knew the name of the guy who owned it, but nobody knew where to find him. I discussed it with a pal and he said: "Oh I know. He drinks in the Uplands Tavern. I'll take you there." So anyhow, I tracked down the owner and he said what he wanted for it and I bought it.

Stefan: So, it was after buying the chalet on Hareslade that you started doing work for people with chalets?

Owen: Yes, I can't remember having done any beforehand [apart from for my father]. Obviously, I had to design one for myself. People were beginning to talk about sustainability and that sort of thing – probably started by yourself amongst others [Laughter]. And so, I actually designed it, about twenty years ago in a way that might have been considered as sustainable then. I don't think they'd invented solar panels that far back, they might have done. I got many commissions after that, not only in Hareslade, but also in some of the other chalet fields. Not necessarily designing new ones, but alternations and extensions that people needed planning permission for. A lot had been rebuilt as really boring brick bungalows filling as much of the plot as they could with barely a meter spare all the way round, with maybe just two meters between the back wall and the boundary - so at least you could step outside! Quite how they got planning permission... they were so far removed from what the Design Guide said. I used some of these boring brick bungalows several times as examples in applications I was doing to discredit the old Design Guide because, although it was still current, I would point out that what I was trying to do in a particular project was more in keeping with the ethos of the old chalets compared to what had been approved so often.

That particularly applied to one, the first one you meet as you go into Hareslade – in the front field – that had been rebuilt as a brick bungalow with Georgian style bow windows on the front and a shallow pitch roof [See adjacent page]. The owner had been an old lady who had been living there forever. I think she'd lived there in an original wooden one before the brick one. But the new owner has had the roof taken off and we put a new forty-five degree pitched roof on, with Velux windows, but they wouldn't allow us to put windows in the gables. In spite of the rules she did, but she put the cladding boards across them. There was a cut-out where you could open the window shutters which appeared to be part of the clap-board sidings.

I have tried to persuade a few people to apply to put some balconies in, to have a steep roof and recess the balcony in from the front. In a traditional chalet, you typically have the veranda at the front with a glazed roof. You replace that roof with an extension of the first floor to make a balcony. It would still appear to be a single floor dwelling with a big roof. This is what I mean when I argue that this sort of rebuild is much more in keeping with the original chalets. The front field has a nice sea view especially if you can go up to that extra level.

The lady at Number 1 decided not to apply for the balcony and risk having the hassle of going through planning refusals... I did try with a second one in the back field, which was one that had been rebuilt previously in timber. We did something similar and took the roof off and replaced it with a much steeper pitch roof - they didn't want the hassle of risking refusals either. And then I got a commission for another - plot 9 - on the front field where the owner lived in a very, very poor one. It was an original chalet but not much of the original was left. It had just been patched with bits of old timber and all sorts of stuff. It was in very poor condition and little character left in it, although it was quite pleasant inside. He was a carpenter and had been there twenty odd years and kept promising himself to rebuild it. So, I tried to persuade him to go for my design, which I'm sure would have been a winner. He was tempted, but wasn't sure he wanted the hassle, so in the end I said: "Well, let's put it in and if it gets refused, which it probably will, I'll put the appeal in and if you lose the appeal I won't charge you." I was convinced that it was a winning formula! So that's what happened. At first, we were refused planning permission. I then appealed [to the Welsh Assembly Government Planning Inspectorate] and we won on appeal. Although this hadn't been built yet, the next-door chalet number 10 changed hands soon afterwards – it had been an old original one.

Owen: The new owner, Pete, who bought that was known to me. His long-term girlfriend had actually been a student of architecture, but she wasn't confident enough to design it so I was asked to do that.

Ironically, Pete was a bricklayer by trade, but he opted for a timber build. That was almost a clone of the one designed at Number 9. It went straight through planning with the recessed balcony. It's built now.

If the planning authority have lost an appeal there's no way they are going to refuse something virtually identical in the same situation... So, you know, the precedent has been set by the Planning Inspectorate that it's acceptable. So, there are quite a few now in Hareslade opening up their hidden first floor gable windows and things...

I've done quite a lot of alterations and extensions to various ones... too many to count!

This one is 'taking liberties' with the guidelines and fell foul of the planning inspectors for a while - although in the end they relented and drew back from a demolition order!

This is Matt's chalet. The following pages show the interior.

Hareslade Community Noticeboard

Afterwords

This book is intended to convey the unique quality of plotland chalets as they morph and change with the times. It is this dynamic adaptation that proves to me their enduring value in the housing landscape.

A link to the full interview with the architect Owen Short.

http://stefan-szczelkun.blogspot.co.uk/2017/10/interview-with-owen-short-august-2015.html

The link to an album of all the Gower photographs.

https://www.flickr.com/gp/stefan-szczelkun/pa8f1X

In England the Chalet developments are known as the Plotlands. I wrote a chapter on the UK Plotlands in my book *The Conspiracy of Good Taste*.

http://www.stefan-szczelkun.org.uk/taste/CGTindex.html

A free ebook can be downloaded here:

http://payhip.com/b/pCoZ

There is a Flickr group that has photos of the many other plotlands all over the UK. This was a widespread phenomenon, active from the Twenties until it was repressed by the 1948 Planning Act.

https://flic.kr/g/j2fwL

Interview transcript by Howard Slater. Thanks to Jess Farr for accommodation in Swansea.

Back cover a view of Stonefields chalet field, Gower.

I first became aware of the plotlands in 1971 when on a tour of the NE of England with the Scratch Orchestra. This was Ovingham – shown below. Soon afterwards I took some slides of chalets on the Gower – see following pages.

The Gower c1972

www.ingramcontent.com/pod-product-compliance
Lightning Source LLC
Chambersburg PA
CBHW041217240426
43661CB00012B/1074